Planet Earth

Hema Vijay

Prodigy

Planet Earth

First Edition: December 2009
64 Pages
Printed in India.

ISBN 978-81-8493-350-5
Pro-ya-en-62

Prodigy Books
177/103, First Floor, Ambal's Building
Lloyds Road, Royapettah, Chennai 600 014.
Ph: +91-44-4200-9603
Email: support@nhm.in
Website: www.nhm.in

Prodigy Books is an imprint of New Horizon Media Pvt. Ltd.

Content

Spaceship Earth

You might never have thought of it this way, but you are a SPACE TRAVELLER!

You are whirling through space! And your space ship – planet EARTH. The ground under your feet may seem stationary, but along with you, the entire planet and all the living creatures on it are on a space voyage, and rotating and revolving around the sun too – all at the same time!

Sounds dizzying, doesn't it?

But then, we don't sense this movement, as we are bound to the ground under our feet by the Earth's gravitational pull.

Of course, you are not zipping through space alone. We, on planet Earth, are moving along with the solar system as a whole, along a path that seems to be stretching ahead endlessly, blasted off into motion by the Big Bang or the great explosion that started the universe.

Our base in space - planet Earth, has been a wonderful home for us. We live on a spectacular planet. A planet that has within it seas and oceans, icy plains and sandy deserts, and many, many, interesting places and features.

But how did the Earth become like this? When was it born? What could happen to Earth in the future? Why are we humans living on planet Earth and not on Mars or Venus? Want to know more about it all? Read on.

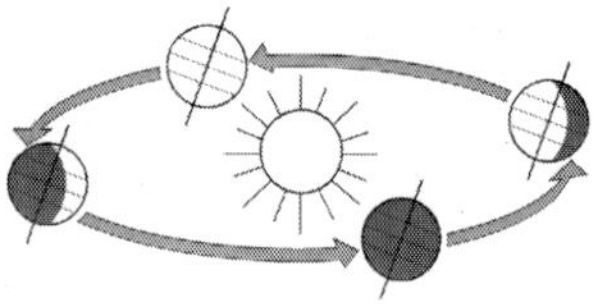

The Earth takes 365.26 days to go once around the sun, at an average speed of 29.78 km/s. This time makes our year.

Place in Space

So, here you are, reading this, probably cocooned in a cosy chair that rests firmly on the surface of this massive sphere that is whirling through space!

Our Earth is the fifth largest of the eight planets in the solar system. But as the bigger planets like Neptune and Uranus are gaseous, the Earth is actually the largest of the terrestrial planets in the solar system. For some of us, the Earth seems like the centre of the universe, with the sun, stars and the moon moving around it. Not so long ago, all human beings thought so too, until we learnt by observation and experiments about our place in space.

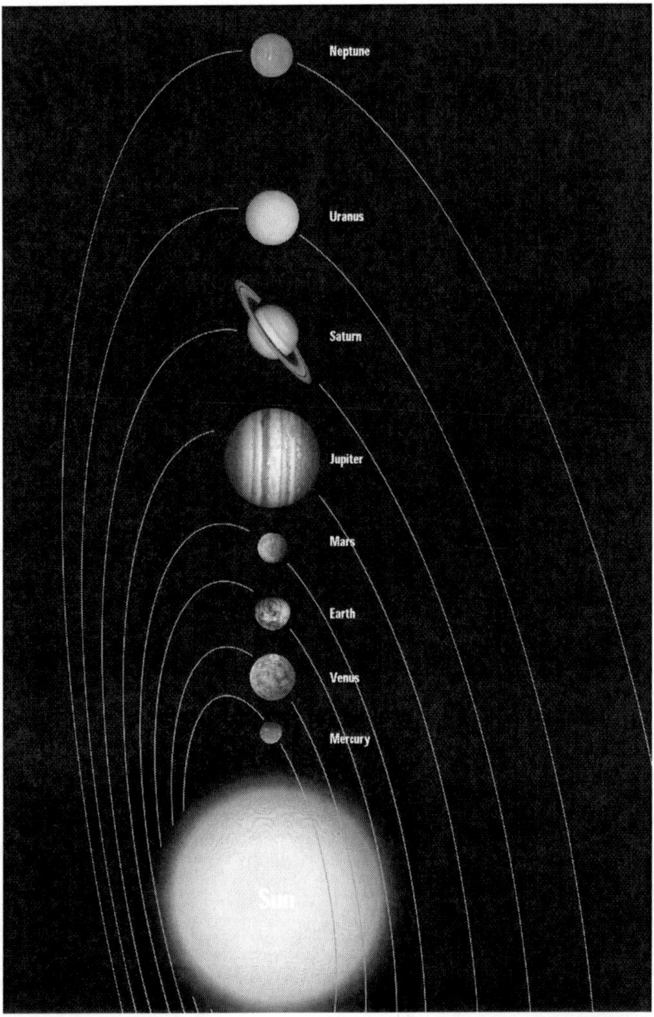
Neptune
Uranus
Saturn
Jupiter
Mars
Earth
Venus
Mercury
Sun

To us, for whom Earth is not only home but also the only planet we have been on, it is a fantastic and fabulous planet, one like no other place on the universe. And indeed, Earth could be a very special planet. Even from space, Earth looks strikingly beautiful - the bright green hues of its plant life, the blue-green tint of the oceans, the brown of its sandy deserts and the white of its icy mountains. Other planets that man has observed seem monotonous and dull by comparison.

Earth in the universe

An alien from another part of the universe would find it difficult to even spot the Earth in the first place. Even if he could zoom in on our planet from among the countless heavenly bodies in space, to an alien observer, the Earth would seem to be a very ordinary planet - a spherical planet that looked like a blue marble, flanked by a tiny white body that we know as the Moon.

Even assuming that this alien had been told that planet Earth with its amazing life forms exists in the universe, he would find it very difficult to locate us, as the Earth is tucked away in a corner of the universe.

To zoom in our planet, the alien would have to first turn his gaze on to the observable part of our massive universe, and then zoom in on the large scale structures in it. He then has to narrow his focus to the Virgo Super Cluster and then on to the group of galaxies called the Local Group within this super cluster. Within the Local Group he has to focus on the Orion arm of the Milky Way Galaxy. Then he has to look for the Gould belt in Orion arm, and then the Local Bubble in the belt, and then to the Local Interstellar Cloud, which has our solar system towards its edge. And finally on to the third planet that revolves around the central star of this solar system. Whew! The alien could easily miss our planet, as you see.

You will have to understand that the Local Interstellar Cloud itself has thousands of stars with solar systems in it and it is a very tiny place in the Milky Way Galaxy. The Milky Way galaxy is orbiting about 28,000 light years from the centre of the galaxy, and you will realize that our home planet is a tiny speck in an obscure spot in the universe. For the alien seeing our planet from a distance, Earth could seem a nondescript planet in a non-prominent part of the universe, one among the countless bodies in space.

But then of course, to us, Earth is very special indeed. It is our home, after all.

Birth of the Earth

Lets take a trip on time machine to the universe as it was before billions of years.

There was no Earth or moon then, not even the Sun. There was just a mass of gas, dust and rock that was swirling around the outer edge of the galaxy. Because of the pull of gravitational force that acts on all particles, this mass of gas came together to form ball-like clusters, which grew bigger and bigger to form stars. One of these stars was our Sun. The disk-shaped mass of dust and gas that was left over slowly came together, attracted by gravity, out of which the planets, moons, asteroids, and other small Solar System bodies formed. Scientists call this process as accretion, and this process took 10 to 20 million years. Our Solar System came into existence some 4.54 billion years ago.

After these particles came together as the Earth, the molten outer layer of the planet cooled to form a solid crust. And all the while when the solid crust was being formed, water was accumulating in Earth's atmosphere. The moon was also being formed almost simultaneously – 4.53 billion years ago. Astrophysicists think that the moon was formed because of a Mars-sized object (scientists have named it Theia) that hit the Earth. Some of Theia's mass merged with the Earth, while a portion of it started orbiting around Earth, becoming our planet's natural satellite, which we have named 'Moon'.

Over time, gases were given off from the Earth's surface, especially from volcanoes. This, and the condensing water vapour above the Earth's surface contributed to Earth's atmosphere.

Meanwhile, ice and liquid water was also being delivered to the Earth by asteroids and some larger proto-planets,

A Light Year: One Light Year is the distance travelled by sunlight in one year, at the speed of (light) 300,000 km per second. Now, calculate what this means. Right, one light year is equal to 9,500,000,000,000 km!

comets, and trans-neptunian objects. This accumulated to form Earth's oceans.

Faint Young Sun paradox

At that point of time, our sun, which had also been formed newly then, was just 70% as bright as it is now. But there was a lot of solar activity in the Sun then. There was also a large volume of greenhouse gases in the atmosphere then; this kept our oceans liquid, despite the fact that the sun was much fainter and was emitting less heat by way of radiation.

Continents and Supercontinents

Now we know about how oceans came to be, but how about our continents? Well, there are two possible ways it could have happened - by steady growth, or by rapid growth early on in Earth's history. Of the two possibilities, what is more likely to have happened is a rapid early growth leading to the formation of a continental crust, followed by a steady increase in the continental area.

The Earth is slightly flattened along the pole-to-pole axis. Scientists say that this bulge at the equator is because of the rotation of the Earth.

Over hundreds of millions of years, the Earth's surface continually reshaped itself, breaking and reforming, sliding across, and sometimes combining together to form supercontinents. Imagine! No continents, no islands, just one solid mass of a supercontinent; the world was literally one then!

The first of these has been nicknamed Rodinia. About 750 million years ago, this supercontinent broke apart and then came together again about 600 to 540 million years ago to form supercontinent Pannotia.

This too broke up and then came together later to form Pangea (meaning *all lands*). Then Pangea too broke apart about 200 million years ago into pieces which drifted apart and became the present-day continents.

Zip to the centre

At a glance, the Earth seems like a solid, homogenous, sphere. But actually, if you could pierce through it and travel to the centre of the planet, you would find a number of different zones and layers. Get strapped for this exciting journey...

A layered planet

Truly, the Earth has layers of personality! Let us begin from the surface. The outermost layer of the Earth, called the crust is mostly composed of silica. The thickness of the crust varies; the crust under the oceans is about 6 km thick, while the crust of the continents is between 30–50 km thick. Under the crust is a curious structure - a highly viscous(sticky) but solid thing called the mantle.

We refer to the crust and the cold, rigid, top of the upper mantle together as the lithosphere. The dynamic tectonic plates, which we will learn about later, are located here. Then there is the Mohorovičić discontinuity or the Moho, the stretch between the Earth's crust and its mantle. The mantle is not a uniform structure. Its structure changes greatly, so that the lower mantle is quite different from the upper mantle. Beneath the mantle is an extremely low viscosity liquid called the outer core, which lies above a solid inner core. This inner core is a very dynamic structure and rotates at a slightly higher angular velocity than the rest of the planet!

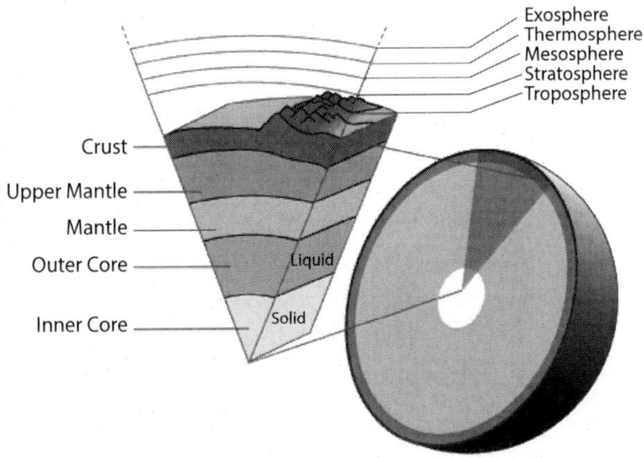

Earth and atmosphere cutaway illustration

Moving plates: When the Earth trembles

The lithosphere is not continuous, but in the form of pieces called tectonic plates, which slide across. Sometimes the plates come together, and in other cases they move apart, sometimes, they even slide past one another in opposite directions!

We hear of earthquakes, and see images on television of high buildings and houses crumbling down. And like wise, earthquakes happen when parts of Earth's crust move or slide past each other and there is too much tension at points where these plates meet. Scientists say that earthquakes are a reminder and warning from nature that we are living on the fragile and thin outer crust of our planet, while the inside of it is still very active, though it is cooling down.

Not just earthquakes, these moving plates also cause volcanic activity, and formation of fold mountains on the continents, or mid oceanic ridges and trenches in the oceans. All this happens along the tectonic plate boundaries, when the plates slide towards each other, collide and rise upwards or downwards, because of lack of space.

The Indian plate, the Australian plate (which fused with the Indian plate about 50-55 million years ago), the Arabian

> Indonesia, Japan, and the United States have the greatest number of active volcanoes.

plate, the Caribbean plate, the Nazca Plate (west coast of South America), the Scotia plate (in the South Atlantic ocean) are the major tectonic plates. Among plates, the oceanic plates are fastest, and the Cocos oceanic plate actually moves at a speed of 75 mm every year; the plate that moves slowest is the Eurasian Plate (21 mm/yr).

Hot facts

Did you know? Not just in the sun, heat is produced in the Earth too. This is called geothermal energy and today, scientists are even trying to tap this heat, to use it as a source of energy. The interior areas of the Earth are extremely active and the centre of the planet is extremely hot and can measure up to as much as 7,000 K. The pressure in this region is very high too, and could reach 360 Gpa. Tectonophysicists use the gigapascal (GPa) in measuring or calculating tectonic forces within the earth.

Some of the heat does escape from the inner regions of the earth. The crust regions under the oceans allow more loss

Tsunami: An earthquake can a tsunami when it originates under the ocean. Near the earthquake's epicenter, the sea floor rises and falls, pushing all the water above it up and down. This produces a huge tidal wave, called a tsunami. Tsunamis can reach uptp 100 feet high. Since 1945, more people have been killed as a result of tsunamis than as a direct result of an earthquake's ground-shaking.

of heat than the crust layers of the continent. The highest temperature recorded at the surface of the earth is 57.7^{0}C, while lowest is -89^{0}C, at the poles.

Magnetic Earth

The Earth is a magnet, by itself! The Earth's magnetic field has its magnetic poles located near the geographic north and south poles. Now, just why does Earth have this magnetic nature?

Well, some scientists think that the magnetic field is generated within the molten outer core region. As we know, in this region, there is a lot of heat, which creates movements called convection motions, which generates electric currents, which in turn produce the Earth's magnetic field. This magnetic field is called the magnetosphere, which has an extremely large reach.

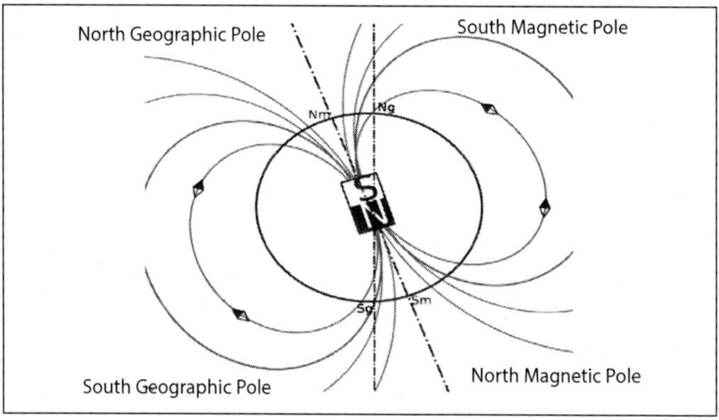

The variation between magnetic north and "true" north.

Elements of the Earth

If you could weigh the Earth, you would find that it weighs 5.98×10^{24} kg. And this includes the weight of the water on Earth.

The solid part of our planet consists mostly of iron (32.1%), oxygen (30.1%), silicon (15.1%), magnesium (13.9%), sulfur (2.9%), nickel (1.8%), calcium (1.5%), and aluminium (1.4%); the remaining 1.2% is from trace amounts of other elements.

Scientists have also found that the deep core region of the Earth is basically composed of iron (88.8%). On the other hand, about 47% of the Earth's crust is constituted by oxygen. What we know as rocks are mostly oxides of various elements such as silica, alumina, iron oxides, lime, magnesia, potash and soda.

Of course, sediments get accumulated on the surface of continents, forming sedimentary rocks. But apart from this, the rocks found in the crust regions of continents are mainly igneous rocks, granite and andesite which are rather less dense, and a little of basalt (a volcanic rock). However, the crust at the bottom of oceans has lots of basalt. Then, there are the metamorphic rocks, which have been transformed from other rock types by the action of high pressure, and or heat.

Planet Earth

Before life appeared on the Earth, the Earth was a totally different kind of place, quite unrecognizable from what it is now. The changes happened because of asteroid impacts, erosion by wind and waves, and the action of living forms that started living on Earth and interacting with the environment.

If all the planets in the world were to be analysed, we might perhaps find that no other planet shows such amazing geographic diversity as our Earth. Icy poles, sandy deserts, wet and slushy marshes, dense rainforests.... We have a lot to be grateful for, haven't we? Imagine one uniform mass of a planet, with every place on it having the same climate and geography. Then there wouldn't be much fun in travelling, right?

Drop of life

Liquid water is a unique feature on Earth, though India's pride, Chandrayan, has just discovered traces of it in moon. About 71% of the Earth's surface is covered with water. And our oceans are incredibly deep. Actually, the average depth of the oceans is 3,800 m, which is more than four times the average height of the continents!

Probably, the Earth would have been uninhabitable, had it not been for this abundance of liquid water.

The deepest underwater location is Challenger Deep of the Mariana Trench in the Pacific Ocean. Its depth goes down to 10,911.4! This trench goes deeper down than the length that Mount Everest rises up to.

The Earth has an ocean volume of 1.4×10^9 km^3. To understand the hugeness of this volume, just suppose that the land on Earth is uniformly flat and spread all across the globe, then the oceanic waters of the Earth would be about 2.7 km high all over the globe. Now that is a large amount of water, isn't it?

Well, you would be carrying water bottles to school. Aren't they heavy? Right, so all this mass of water by way of oceans would weigh a lot. The oceans of the world, put together, weigh about 1.4×10^{18} metric tons. This weight is about 1/4400 of the total mass of the Earth. Salt contributes about 3.5% of the total weight of oceanic water. Just 2.5% of the water on Earth is salt free, and of that too, about 68.7% is in the form of ice. So fresh water is a scarce commodity, and we need to avoid wasting it.

We see the seas and oceans as flat masses of water, broken perhaps by waves and tides. But actually, the crust under the ocean waters has many land forms ranging from mountains, the long mid-oceanic ridge, undersea volcanoes, canyons, trenches, plateaus and plains.

> Nearly 70 percent of the Earth's fresh-water supply is locked up in the icecaps of Antarctica and Greenland. The remaining exists in the atmosphere, streams, lakes, or groundwater. This accounts for a mere 1 percent of the Earth's total fresh-water supply.

How did the ocean become salty?

We know that little of the water was formed by reactions on the surface of the Earth, while plenty more was brought to the Earth by crashing asteroids from space. This water must initially have been fresh water or salt free. How did this water become salty? Well, some of the salt was released from the rocks and sediments of the Earth's crust from volcanic activity, while the rest came from igneous rocks. Apart from salt, the ocean also has atmospheric gases dissolved in it. This is crucial for the survival of aquatic organisms.

This large volume of oceanic water is a blessing for us, as it helps to regulate the temperature of the Earth. Oceanic water can sponge in a lot of heat and so act as a heat reservoir, without which many places on Earth would have become intolerably hot.

Gas giants: Only Mercury, Venus, Earth, and Mars are solid. The rest of the planets - Jupiter, Saturn, Uranus, and Neptune are just gas, with no solid stuff for you to rest your feet on!

The invisible friend

You might not have thought much about the air. Out of sight, out of mind, isn't it? But, our existence owes a great deal to the Earth's atmosphere, or what we commonly call 'air'.

Like an invisible friend, Earth's atmosphere helps us in many ways. Obviously, it allows the water cycle by which water evaporates (in the heat of the sun's rays) from the ocean and other water bodies and falls down as pure, fresh water. That apart, the air also ensures that the small meteors which keep falling down towards the Earth get burnt up in the atmosphere itself because of friction. If meteors fall down on Earth as they are, there would have been as many craters (and so many accidents, too, were the meteors to fall on any of us) on Earth, as on the moon.

Our atmosphere has a hand in moderating our planet's surface temperature too, circulating hot and cold air around the globe. Then, there is the greenhouse effect. Now of course, we are suffering from an overdose of the greenhouse effect; but we do need some amount of greenhouse effect if the Earth is to be habitable.

Do you know how the greenhouse effect happens? As in a greenhouse made of glass in cold countries, the molecules of carbon dioxide, water vapor, methane, ozone, etc in the atmosphere trap the heat energy from the sun. Otherwise all the sunlight would get reflected back into space.

If this sunlight had not been trapped by the atmosphere, then Earth would have been a very cold, frozen place indeed, without liquid water. Liquid water is where life first started to evolve. Scientists estimate that without this greenhouse effect, the average surface temperature would be 18 °C.

> Without the gravitational pull of the Earth, Earth would have no atmosphere; gases in the air would all have floated away into space. But then, so would we!

The planet's first pollutant

The air on Earth is quite different from what it was when Earth was formed. Actually, it is the life forms on Earth which have changed its composition.

Guess what was the first pollutant on Earth? To know the answer to that we have to go back in time and understand the nature of the air on primitive Earth. Primitive Earth had no oxygen.

Some 2.7 billion years ago, plant forms started absorbing carbon dioxide and started giving out oxygen; in other words, photosynthesis evolved on Earth. Over a period of time, the concentration of oxygen in the Earth's atmosphere gradually increased because of continued photosynthesis. It was only later that the Earth saw the emergence of oxygen-breathing life forms.

Later, this oxygen in the atmosphere formed ozone (oxygen with three atoms, unlike the oxygen with two atoms that we absorb when we breathe in). The ozone accumulated and gradually formed a layer high up in the atmosphere. This was a lucky development, as the ozone layer is our shield against the harmful ultraviolet radiations from the sun.

Currently, our atmosphere has a large concentration of nitrogen (78.08%). Oxygen comes next with a concentration of 20.95%. There is also a little of argon (0.93%), and carbon dioxide (0.038%). There is about 1% of water vapour in the atmosphere too, but its concentration changes according to the climate at that point of time.

Edge of the Earth

Actually, it is difficult to pinpoint just where Earth's atmosphere ends. It just gradually becomes thinner and thinner and becomes non-existent further up. But generally, the Karman line, an imaginary line in the atmosphere at a distance of 100km above the Earth's surface is considered the limit or boundary between Earth's atmosphere and space.

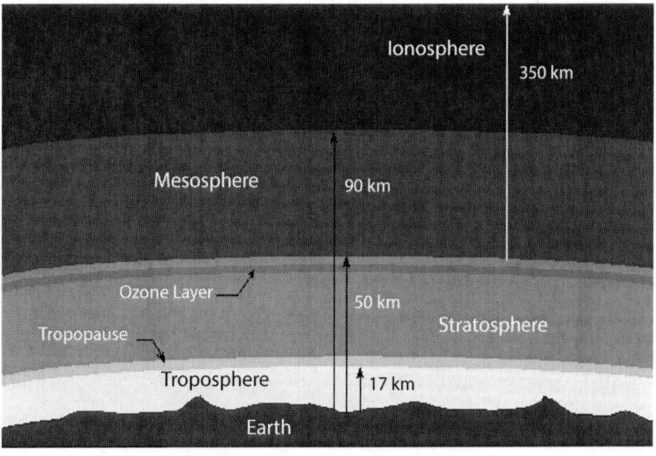

Three fourths of the entire weight of the atmosphere is found within the first 17 km of the planet's surface. This 17 km width of atmosphere is what meteorologists (people who study climate patterns) call the troposphere. When this layer of air is heated by sunlight, the air expands and rises up. Cooler air, which happens to be heavier too, rushes in to fill this space. This brings about a circulation of air, or what we commonly called wind. Otherwise, our atmosphere would be still, without winds or breezes.

The thin layers of atmosphere beyond a height of 17 km from the Earth's surface contain the stratosphere (where lies the ozone layer that shields us from ultraviolet radiations from the sun), followed by the mesosphere and the thermosphere layers of the atmosphere. The thermosphere includes the exosphere and part of the ionosphere. Our atmosphere becomes cooler with increasing height, because of less and less particles available there to trap the heat from

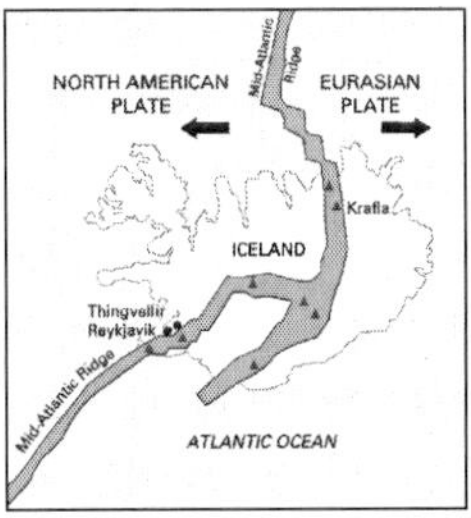

The longest mountain chain on Earth is the Mid-Atlantic Ridge. It is about 40,000 km and splits nearly the entire Atlantic Ocean north to south. Iceland is one place where this submarine mountain chain rises above the sea surface.

the sun. Beyond the mesosphere is the exosphere, followed by the magnetosphere region, where the magnetic field of the Earth reacts with the solar wind.

Earth's magnetic field acts as a shield against the solar wind, creating a region called the magnetosphere. Otherwise, the solar wind, which carries deadly electrically charged particles, would harm us. As such, these particles get trapped in the Van Allen Belts, the two bands that circle Earth.

Actually, some of the molecules in the outer edge of Earth's atmosphere are slowly escaping from the gravitational pull of the Earth, all the time, because their velocity has been increased by the absorption of heat energy from the sun. Among these molecules, it is unfixed hydrogen with its low molecular weight, which is most commonly achieving the escape velocity required to move out of the gravitational pull of the Earth.

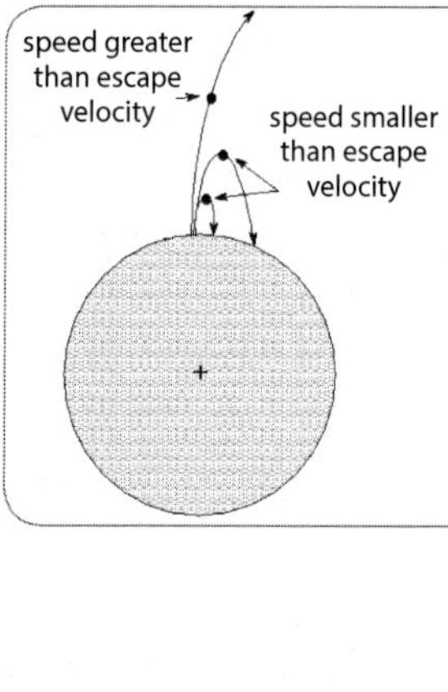

To move out of the Earth's gravitational pull, we need to achieve a velocity of 11.19 km/s. This is termed Earth's escape velocity; so every time you want to launch a rocket into space, you need to give it a thrust of 11.19 km/second.

Wow! That is some speed, isn't it?

Too much of a good thing: Greenhouse effect

The greenhouse effect has helped life evolve on earth, true. But there is such a thing as too much of a good thing. Currently, the temperature of the Earth's surface is rising because of an increase in greenhouse gases (gases like CO_2, CO, etc), which trap heat by not allowing sunlight to be reflected back from the atmosphere. This is alarming. If the temperature continues to rise, the polar ice caps would melt; the melting ice would add to the oceanic volume and this would mean that the oceanic water would rise in height and flow over low lying lands. So watch out, we need to limit our greenhouse gas emissions, otherwise, cities on seacoasts and oceanic islands will go under water, like the famed Dwaraka, Lord Krishna's city, off the coast of Gujarat, which is now under water.

Weatherman's Tales

Imagine a life without daytime alternating with night; if there were no rainy seasons spent splashing about in puddles; no fiery summers when ice creams seem even more delicious than usual; no cold winters when we like to snuggle up in bed and sleep for a little longer. Well, the changing weather and climate spice up life on Earth.

How does it all happen? Why is the climate so different in the same place at different points of time? What makes our years, days and nights, weather and climate?

Day and Year

If we were to calculate in terms of seconds, it takes 86,400 seconds for the Earth to make a complete rotation about its own axis. This time - 24 hours - is what we define as a single day. It takes 365.26 mean solar days for the Earth to complete a single orbital journey around the sun, moving at a speed of 30 km per second. This time defines our year. But such time definitions are planet specific.

Take Mars. Mars takes on an average 24 hours and 39.5 minutes to make a full rotation about its axis; so a Martian day is almost just as long as a day on Earth. But a year on Mars would be almost twice as long as that on Earth, because, Mars takes 687 Earth days to make a complete revolution around the sun.

What tilts the seasons

The Earth's axis is not straight up, but slightly inclined. Earth got this tilt (of 23.5^0) when Theia dashed into Earth about 4.5 billion years ago and the moon was formed. It is this tilt that brings about the seasons: The sunlight falling on the Earth's surface is different at different points of the year, because of the tilted position of the Earth.

The northern hemisphere has summer and the southern hemisphere has winter when the North Pole slants toward the sun. At this point of time, even though the Earth is then at its farthest position from the sun, the sunlight is less slanted and lasts longer. Likewise, winter in the Northern Hemisphere happens when the North Pole tilts away from the Sun and the Southern Hemisphere has its summer.

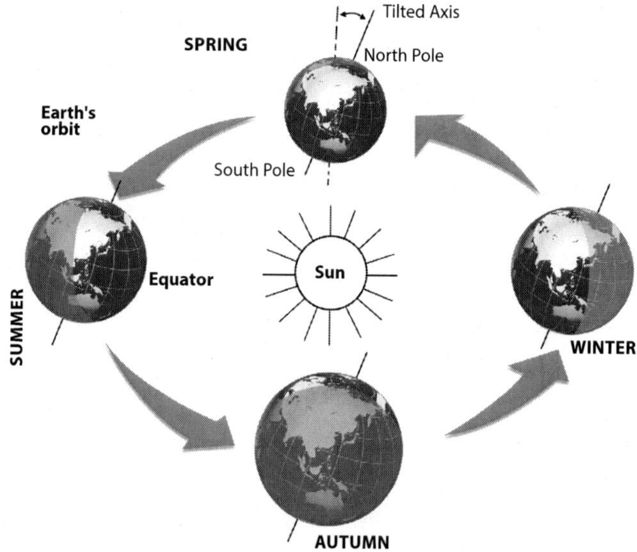

Summer in the northern hemisphere occurs when the North Pole is pointing towards the Sun. Winter occurs in this region when the pole is pointed away from the sun. During summer, the day lasts longer and you can actually notice the sun climbing higher in the sky during summer. During winter, days get shorter of course.

Winds of change

We saw earlier how atmospheric circulation happens. Actually, there are different patterns to it. In the equatorial region below 30^0latitude, the winds operating are called the trade winds; in the mid region, between latitudes 30^0

and 60^0, the winds are called the westerlies. Wind shapes our climate a great deal. They push warm or cold air, like the Northeast and Southwest monsoon winds that bring rain to our country. They have the power to even push storms away or towards a place. No wonder, *Vaayu* the God of Wind, according to Hindu mythology is shown as a powerful being. Winds also cool or warm a place. Sea breezes flowing towards the land cool the coastal areas giving great relief to blazing areas located on the coast like Chennai.

It is a lucky thing for us that we have so much of ocean water on the Earth. The fun of paddling in the waves apart, they are crucial for our survival. Ocean currents carry heat energy that falls on the oceans of the equatorial areas to the polar regions. This circulation of currents, called the thermohaline circulation, plays a crucial role in maintaining the planet's climate. Warm, humid air laden with water vapour brings rain in different parts of the world according to the wind patterns there.

Endless night: At the north pole, and in regions located in the Arctic circle, for instance, the climate is weird. There, part of the year is without any daylight! That is one long night! This is called the polar night. Likewise, at the south pole, and in parts of the Earth in the Antarctic circle, part of the year is without any night. An exact reverse situation.

Yes to Life

The Earth is the only place in the universe where we know for sure that life exists. In fact, life appeared on Earth in the form of tiny microscopic creatures even within a billion years of its formation.

What makes life on Earth possible? Why does the Earth alone have life forms like us human beings while neighbouring planets like Mars are lifeless? Future explorations might discover life forms elsewhere, but still, the Earth is uniquely poised to support life.

Scientists expect that the Earth would continue to support life for another 1.5 billion years, at the end of which time, the increasing luminosity of our sun would restrict and soon extinguish life forms on our planet.

Life on Earth depends on a lot of ifs… without which Earth would not be able to support life. This is what makes our Earth such a special planet. It is just perfectly suited for life. We need to value this blessing and take care of our Earth's environment. Otherwise, all this evolution of life over billions and billions of years can come to a naught.

Unique Earth!

Why is it that we live on the Earth and not on the moon or mars?

Does the question sound foolish? Actually, it is a crucial question, the answer to which holds so much significance. This is because, planet Earth is uniquely suited for life, which allowed life forms to evolve and survive.

Actually, many scientists believe that the universe is full of microbes. Gaseous accumulations between stars can generate amino acids, the building blocks of proteins. Note also that meteors falling to Earth contain many organic compounds. So it is possible that microbes could evolve in space. But for complex life like intelligent human beings with their civilizations and communication capacities to evolve, it takes much more. We don't know if these set of conditions are seen elsewhere in the universe.

Evolution of life depends on a unique combination of factors, like the ones that happened on our Earth. For example, the existence of tectonic plates; when they slide past one another, carbon dioxide is pushed to the surface. This carbon dioxide created the green house effect, without which Earth would have been a lifeless, frozen sphere, perhaps like Pluto.

And to survive long enough for complex life forms to evolve, the planet should not suffer any massive meteor impact too. For planet Earth, Jupiter has played a guardian angel, as Jupiter's gravitational field slows down incoming space debris like comets. In other solar systems, it is likely that such Jupiter-sized planets, if present, would be having erratic orbits, and would not be able to shield space debris consistently.

And if the Earth revolved much faster than its current speed, the planet's centrifugal force would pull it away from the sun. This too would have made Earth too frozen and cold for life. And if Earth revolved slower, then, it

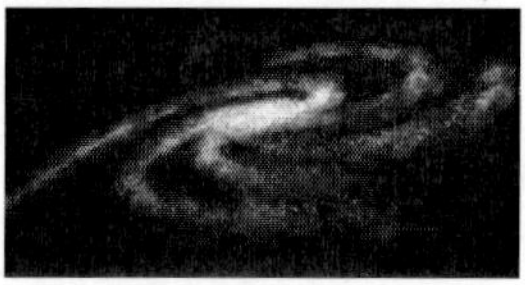

The Milky Way Galaxy is a spiral galaxy that contains roughly 200 billion stars. Our solar system is located in the outer reaches of the Milky Way Galaxy.

would be pulled closer to the sun, and so be too hot for life, like Mercury. And just supposing the moon were nearer to our Earth, tides would be more massive and cover the surface of the planet with water to a depth of over 2 km.

If Earth did not have so much liquid water, which has a balancing effect on temperature, then day and night temperatures would vary too drastically to allow for complex life to evolve. Speaking of water, if it did not have the nature of being lighter in its frozen form of ice, then, the oceans would start freezing from bottom up winter after winter, and eventually make the planet too frozen and barren for life! As it is, frozen water is lighter than ice and stays on the surface, keeping the water underneath it warm enough for oceanic creatures to survive.

Then, there is our invisible friend, the atmosphere, which burns up falling meteors and save us from massive impacts. So, if our planet had been just a little further away or closer to the sun, if she did not take an elliptical orbit around

The tallest point on Earth is the Mount Everest (8,848 m above sea level) and the lowest point of the Earth's terrestrial surface is Mariana Trench (10,911 m below sea level).

the sun and rotate at this speed; if she hadn't been tilted along her axis, if she did not have this magnetic field, this atmosphere… if any of the conditions mentioned above had been even slightly different, then life as we see it now would not have been possible on Earth.

But then of course, life has a capacity to makes its own way, whatever be the condition. So who knows! And hmm... did you notice any extra terrestrial life around you?

Best Friends

If our planet could name its best friend, guess what she would say? Right. "The Moon". The moon, quite literally is planet Earth's constant companion. No wonder that so many poems have been composed around the moon. Earth's moon provides the Earth with ocean tides, stabilizes the planet's axial tilt, thereby stabilizing the planet's climate, and gradually slows the planet's rotation. Not only that, in a psychological sense, the moon has contributed a great deal to man's fascination and exploration of space. If not for the moon, some scientists think that we would not have as easily made our first landing in space. The moon gave us a launching pad for our leap into space; friendly neighbourhood to test our visit into space.

No other planet in our solar system has a satellite so close to its own size, apart from Pluto and its satellite Charon.

In fact, some scientists regard the Earth-Moon system as a double planet system. The moon orbits around the Earth once every 27 days, 7 hours and 43.7 minutes. The Moon is about 384,000 km away from us. Not too far away at all, when distances in space are considered.

This sense of comfort apart, the moon has a practical role in helping us Earthlings live comfortably. Let us begin with tides. It is the gravitational attraction between the Earth and the moon that causes our tides. That is why the tides are always at their highest during full moon and new moon days. Actually, because of this tidal interaction, the moon is very slowly moving away from the Earth, at a speed of 38mm a year.

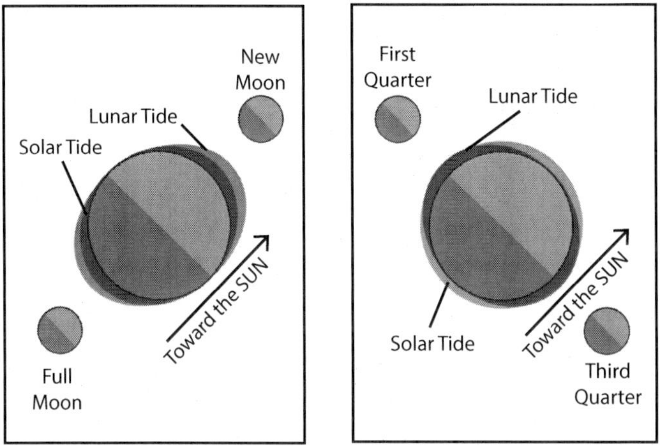

Motion of tidal bulges created by the Moon

As the moon comes round the Earth, the sunlight falls in a specific pattern on it, from no illumination at all (new moon) to illuminating the entire face of the moon (full moon), in a cyclical pattern. This is what we refer to as the phases of the moon or lunar phases.

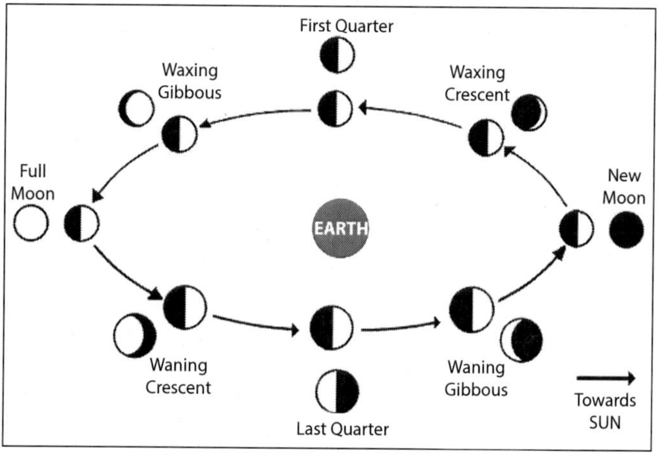

Phases of the Moon

The silent giver

We learn a lot from observing our parents and teachers, right? We can learn a lot from the silent Earth, too.

The Earth is a master recycling machine, for instance. Would you believe that it is the heat and pressure within the Earth that turned organic waste into our petroleum fuel and natural gas, and even diamonds? Well, we must be careful about how we use this bounty that the Earth has made for us, as we don't know how to make petroleum, as of now. There are some scientists who are trying to simulate these heat and pressure conditions to create artificial petroleum; but matching up to Earth's level of expertise is a tall order, right?

It is Earth which set the stage for plant life to manufacture our food, wood, medicines, not to mention oxygen that our lives depend on now. Move over to minerals. Erosion and plate tectonics has given rise to mineral ores which we melt and get our metals like iron and aluminium, and non-metallic elements like silica, which are key to our mechanized and appliance based lives of today.

How many of us

Do you know how many people live on Earth now? It was no less than 6,740,000,000, even back in November 2008. Now of course, it must have increased by a leap. Demographers, or people who study populations, predict that the number of people living on Earth would be seven billion in 2013 and 9.2 billion in 2050!

But remember, this human population is wedged in niches. Only about an eighth of the surface of the Earth is habitable by man. As you know, three quarters of Earth's surface is covered by oceans. Of the remaining quarter, half of it consists of deserts (14%) and high mountains (27%), or extreme areas like the poles. It is a tribute to man's capacity for survival that he has managed to venture and even establish a permanent base at barren and frozen places like the poles - such as the Amundsen-Scott South Pole Station at the South Pole!

As our population keeps increasing, we will have to think of new areas to live on. Space explorations could hold the key. Already, scientists are seriously thinking of setting up living bases in the moon. With the Chandrayan having discovered liquid water on the moon, this might happen sooner than later. How about you? Wouldn't you like to visit the moon?

Microbes to Monkeys

Planet Earth is uniquely suited for sustaining life forms. But how did it all begin?

For this, we need to go back in time. Rewind back to the earth as it was four billion years ago. It was a time when there was a lot of radiation coming into the Earth; it was a thrilling time when the atmosphere was very violent. This huge energy in the air somehow triggered the formation of a self-replicating molecule - a molecule that is able to produce copies of itself! Scientists believe that it happened in the oceans of primitive Earth, which they call the primordial soup of life.

The next crucial step was the development of photosynthesis, which meant that these primordial forms could directly tap solar energy; photosynthesis also meant that the atmosphere was becoming more and more oxygenated and some of it even reacted among themselves to form a layer of protective ozone.

Later, complex interactions among these particles produced the first primitive cells. This was followed by the emergence of complex cells. Some of these complex cells somehow started aggregating into groups for better survival, leading to the formation of colonies of cells; some of these colonies became more and more specialized and formed the first multi-cellular organisms. Over time, more and more complex forms kept emerging, and now, here we are, human beings - organisms so complex that we dare to wonder about how we came to be!

All this didn't happen at a uniform pace. There were times when not much evolution happened; at other times, a great number of new creatures burst into life in a short span of time. Alongside, the Earth was also witnessing tumultuous geographical and climatic changes, which too influenced this path of life.

For instance, between 750 and 580 million years ago, the Earth froze because of glacial action and soon came to resemble a giant snowball. When this ice began to thaw, there was an explosion of multi-cellular life forms, which we call the Cambrian explosion. After this, between 535 million years ago and 65 million years ago, there were five mass extinctions, when much of the diverse life forms on Earth were wiped away.

The extinction that happened around 65 million years ago (which we think happened because of a massive meteorite collided with the Earth), was a lucky one for us; because, you see, it wiped off the dinosaurs. If the dinosaurs hadn't been wiped out, perhaps mammals would not have had the freedom or space to evolve so much, and you and I may not be around now to read about the story of the Earth. It was after this extinction event that mammals began to really take control of the world, and eventually, the Earth saw the evolution of intelligent apes which learnt to use tools, culminating in the evolution of us - species Homo sapiens or modern man.

Even after the evolution of man, the Earth saw big ice ages when the Earth froze totally. The last ice age ended 10,000 years ago.

Timeline

Time! We sense time in terms of hours, days, months, and maybe, years. And of course, there are the historians among us who think in terms of centuries too. But for planet Earth, man's time on Earth would seem just a flicker. Humans came into existence just 100,000 years ago, and man's recorded history that spans about 5000 years represents only one millionth (0.00001%) of Earth's lifetime so far. When we talk of Earth's timeline, we count in terms of millions and billions of years.

From a swirling mass of gas to a solid planet on which people like you and me walk and wonder about the universe, events on Earth has been most exciting and magical. If planet Earth had eyes, this is what she would have seen in her lifetime so far.

5 billion years ago: A swirling mass of gas and dust was coming together

4.5 billion years ago: The mass aggregates to form planet Earth, but it was not the solid planet that we stand on now.

3.7 billion years ago: The Earth becomes a solid structure. Slowly, an atmosphere of gases develops around the planet from volcanic gases like methane, ammonia, and hydrogen cyanide. Water condenses and oceans begin to be formed.

3.5 billion years ago: A fabulous thing happens now. The first life appears on Earth in the form of bacteria. And soon, in the oceans, photosynthesis starts occurring.

3 billion years ago: There is a growing rise in the amount of oxygen (given off during photosynthesis) in the atmosphere.

> The exact distance between Earth and the Sun varies with its position in its orbit, which is elliptical. The Earth is on average about 150 million kilometers away from the sun. It is 152 million kilometers away from the sun in the winter and 147 million kilometers away from the sun in the summer.

2.6 billion years ago. Oxygen starts reacting with the planet's crust. Blue green algae emerge in the oceans; these life forms exist on Earth even now.

1.9 billion years ago. First cells with nuclei (called Eukaryotes) appear

650 million years ago: For the first time, Earth sees the evolution of multi-cellular organisms. Hereafter, the pace of evolution on Earth begins to gather speed. In the next 100 million years, lichens appear on land, while multi-cellular life forms in the oceans thrive and become very abundant.

510 million years ago: Another major event happens now; plants emerge on land, with their internal tubes for transporting water. Some 250 years after this, a major extinction event occurs on Earth. We don't know what or how the event happened, but, as a result of this, 99% of all species that existed then on Earth became extinct. But life is all-powerful, and soon, new forms of life emerge on Earth, and eventually, the spectacular dinosaurs appear, took

The distance from the surface of Earth to the center is about 6,378 kilometers. Much of Earth is fluid. The mostly solid skin of the planet is only 66 kilometers thick.

control and ruled the planet. The Earth had been having just one landmass in the form of a super continent Pangea then. Pangea breaks up towards the end of this period.

65 million years ago: The dinosaurs vanish form the face of the Earth. Not just the dinosaurs, about 75% of all species on Earth vanish from Earth and become extinct.

100,000 years ago: Man appears on Earth! So, man has been around for just 100,000 years on Earth, while blue green algae have been living on Earth for the last 2.6 billion years or 2,600,000,000 years!

Some scientists say (only half jokingly) that it is not man, but tiresome insects like mosquitoes, flies, and cockroaches that dominate the world now, as we are unable to control them! In fact, some extraterrestrial life experts even believe that it is insect-like forms that we would likely see in our search for extra terrestrial life, as insects have tough external cover, which could be radiation resistant and help them survive in the high radiation regions of space.

Red Giant

What is going to be our planet's future?

The sun holds a big part of the answer to this question. The brightness and heat of the sun is increasing. The sun's luminosity is expected to increase by 10% over the next 1.1 billion years, and by 40% over the next 3.5 billion years.

This means that there will be a large level of radiation falling on the Earth. This could cause evaporation of the Earth's oceans, among other things. The Earth's surface temperature would also rise, and the global surface temperature could touch 70^{0}C then. This will accelerate the inorganic CO_2 cycle that goes on in our planet, and later drastically reduce the CO_2 concentration in our atmosphere. This would wipe out plant life in about 900 million years. Elimination of animal life would follow it, obviously.

Scientists expect that the Earth would be habitable for about another 500 million more years. So, what does man do after that?

The future

The sun, like other stars will eventually become a reddish tinted giant form, called the 'Red Giant', because of the reactions happening inside it. This would take about five billion years, and our sun would have expanded to about 250 times its present radius.

There is another possibility. Since the Sun will lose about 30% of its mass, the gravitational effects will be less, and the Earth will move away to an orbit 250,000,000 km away from the Sun. But by then, life remaining on the Earth will have been wiped out.

Do you know the astronomical symbol for Earth?
It is a cross circumscribed by a circle.

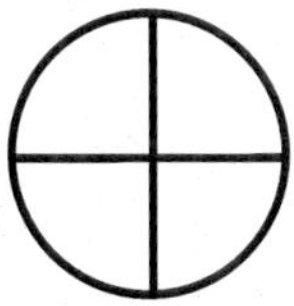

Other scientists think that Earth's orbit could become smaller and that the Earth would eventually be dragged into the red giant Sun's atmosphere and be destroyed.

But hey, don't take this too grimly! If man works sensibly and continues to advance in space technology and exploration, we could have moved to another habitable planet long before this happens.

In fact, global warming, pollution, loss of biodiversity, dwindling freshwater reserves and such environmental issues, not to mention annihilation by nuclear weapons in the event of nuclear war breaking out, pose a greater risk to our survival than astronomical events.

Take care of Earth. Your life depends on her.

Are we alone in the Universe?

Actually, since there are an incredibly large number of stars and planets in the universe, some scientists believe that there must be life elsewhere in the universe, in planets which are conducive to life. In fact, astronomer and astrophysicist Frank Drake suggested in 1960 that the number of communicating civilizations in the Milky Way Galaxy alone would be 10,000!

He put forward an equation that calculates the number of communicating civilizations in galaxies, which became famous as the Drake Equation. The Drake equation states that:

$$N = R^{*} \times f_{p} \times n_{e} \times f_{!} \times f_{i} \times f_{i} \times L$$

where:

N is the number of civilizations in our galaxy with which communication might be possible;

R^* is the average rate of star formation per year in our galaxy.

f_p is the fraction of those stars that have planets.

n_e is the average number of planets that can potentially support life per star that has planets

$f_!$ is the fraction of the above that actually go on to develop life at some point

f_i is the fraction of the above that actually go on to develop intelligent life

f_c is the fraction of civilizations that develop a technology that releases detectable signs of their existence into space

L is the length of time such civilizations release detectable signals into space.

Drake went on to suggest that the reason we have no contacts with extra terrestrial life though a large number of extraterrestrial civilizations would be out there in the universe, is that, highly technological civilizations tend to destroy themselves too quickly before they could make contact with one another!

Flat Earth Days

There was a time when man thought that the Earth was flat; that the Earth was the center of the universe; that the sun, stars and the even the entire universe moved around our planet.

No so very long ago, people thought it self-evident that the Earth was stationary. Well, it does appear so at a casual glance, doesn't it? Now, of course, we know that we are standing on a spherical body whizzing past space.

Myths and facts

We may have moved from some myths and illusions. But we still continue to look upon planet Earth as a 'mother' figure. For instance, Hindus regard the Earth as Bhooma Devi, a consort of Lord Vishnu, and as a divine mother. The Romans called her Terra and also as Tellus.

The Greeks called her Gaia. Greek mythology has its own version of how the Earth evolved. According to Greek mythology, in the beginning, the Earth was a silent bare place, without trees, flowers, grass or birds, when God Eros pierced the cold Earth with his arrows. In an instant, the Earth became verdant and full of life. Then Earth or Gaia, in a rush of happiness and gratitude for this, created Uranus (Heaven, in Greek mythology). In fact, the Greeks felt that their Mount Olympus, the legendary abode of their gods, was the exact centre of the universe! Eventually, our planet got its name from 'erda', an Anglo-Saxon word that means 'ground or soil'.

The dawn of 'Spinning Earth' ideas

But even in early civilizations, there were some people like Eratosthenes, who suspected that our Earth was a sphere, despite how flat it looks to the eye. In fact, this smart man had even calculated Earth's circumference, using just his intelligent deductions, without any technological help!

Then came Aristarchus of Samos (near Turkey) in 200 B.C., who had the courage to tell people that the Earth was not still but spinning all the time. Imagine the reaction his statement would have caused!

Luckily, he was not punished for his radical thinking; but people did not accept his ideas either. They argued that if the Earth were indeed spinning, then people would be thrown off the surface of the Earth; and that birds would have to fly to just stay in the same spot, as the Earth would have moved under them if they remained still. This sounds like common sense, but people then had not understood about Newton's theory of the gravitational force of the Earth that keeps us anchored to the Earth, and about Einstein's theory of relativity, which explains motions of objects on Earth in relation to other moving or stationary objects.

In those times when Aristarchus lived, contradictory sounding new ideas were not welcomed. People who dared to mouth such radical ideas were even punished. So, Aristarchus's idea was slowly buried.

It was a long time before anybody again gathered up the courage to state again that the Earth spins on its own axis. In 1543, Copernicus proclaimed that the Earth spins on its axis as it orbits the sun. Again, his ideas were not accepted. Actually, Copernicus had waited until the end of his life to publish these radical ideas as he feared that he and his ideas would be condemned by the Church, which was an all powerful dictatorial kind of body in those times.

100 years later came Galileo, who gave scientific support to Copernicus's ideas. He used telescopes that he himself

invented and showed people that Venus orbited the sun. His telescopic observations of the phases of Venus looked somewhat like the phases of the moon. The Earth's spinning nature was then proved. So, in effect, popular acceptance of Earth's spinning nature took over 1800 years, after the idea was first suggested.

Then in 1830, Charles Lyell proposed that the Earth evolved gradually, changing over time. This was against the popular belief in all cultures then, which stated that God created the Earth, as it is. Lyell's book, *Principles of Geology: An Attempt to Explain the Former Changes of the Earth's Surface by Reference to Causes Now in Operation* explained how the Earth was shaped by slow-moving forces over a long time.

In 1907, a scientist called Bertram Boltwood decided to use radiometric-dating techniques to calculate the age of the Earth. He figured that the Earth was about 2.2 billion years old. This is not quite right; the Earth is about 4.5 billion years old, but his attempt was stunning in that he gave a lifetime to our planet.

Well, most civilizations around the world had their own versions of how the Earth came to be, and of what it is, in the first place. They were based on imaginative stories about how a creator created the Earth. We regard their beliefs as myths and legends. But modern human beings like us too have our own theories on the Earth, which we surmise from our scientific observations and inferences. But a day might come when these theories are overwritten by some other proof. That is why some philosophers call our theories on the Earth and the universe as the 'new creation myths'.

But whatever the truth may be, the fact remains that we live on a marvellous planet, which has so many mysteries hidden in it, which in turn inspire myths and legends.

We once thought of the Earth as being flat. Slowly, from various observations and oceanic circumnavigation, we understood that the Earth is actually a sphere. In fact, astrophysicists say that this theory could hold true for the concept of time too. Now, we think of time as a straight line going towards the future.

During the summer solstice in the Northern Hemisphere, the Sun is as far north as possible, and hence on this day all places within 23 degrees of the North Pole have constant sunlight. At the South Pole, during this time, there is perpetual night.

During the northern winter solstice, conversely, the North Pole, being tilted away from the Sun, experiences perpetual night, while in the Southern Hemisphere the "midnight Sun" is visible throughout the south polar region.

Some physicists consider that time and space could be two sides of the same coin, and that time could be circular too. Like the flatness of the Earth, the straight line projectory of time could be an illusion too!

Now, with views and new perspectives from spaceflights and other scientific advances, exciting times are ahead as we uncover one thrilling secret about the universe, after another. As Shakespeare had said, "*There are more things in this Universe than are dreamt of in your philosophy.*"

Well, we only know that we know very little. But we are thrilled by this knowledge and are thirsting to know more, and more…

Prodigy books

Biographies

Abdul Kalam
Charles Darwin
Marie Curie
Visvesvaraya
Srinivasa Ramanujan
Newton
Einstein
James Watt
Sir JC Bose
Alexander Graham Bell
Gandhi
Jawaharlal Nehru
Mother Teresa
Ambedkar
Bhagat Sigh
Tipu Sultan
Rani of Jhansi
Akbar
Shivaji
Bharati
Rabindranath Tagore
Martin Luther King
Alexander the Great
Napoleon
Adolf Hitler
Charlie Chaplin
Walt Disney
Bill Gates
Narayana Murthy
Columbus

Classics Retold

Homer's Iliad
The Odyssey
The Tempest
Hamlet
The Merchant of Venice
Twelfth Night
Romeo and Juliet
Macbeth

Other Titles

The Universe
Hinduism
Global Warming
Abraham Lincoln
The New 7 wonders of the World
Life
Tsunami
Dinosaurs
Ganga
World War II
Madras - Chennai
Exam Tips
Television
Effective Communication
Creative Thinking